AMAZING MIGRATIONS

ON THE MOVE WITH CARIBOU

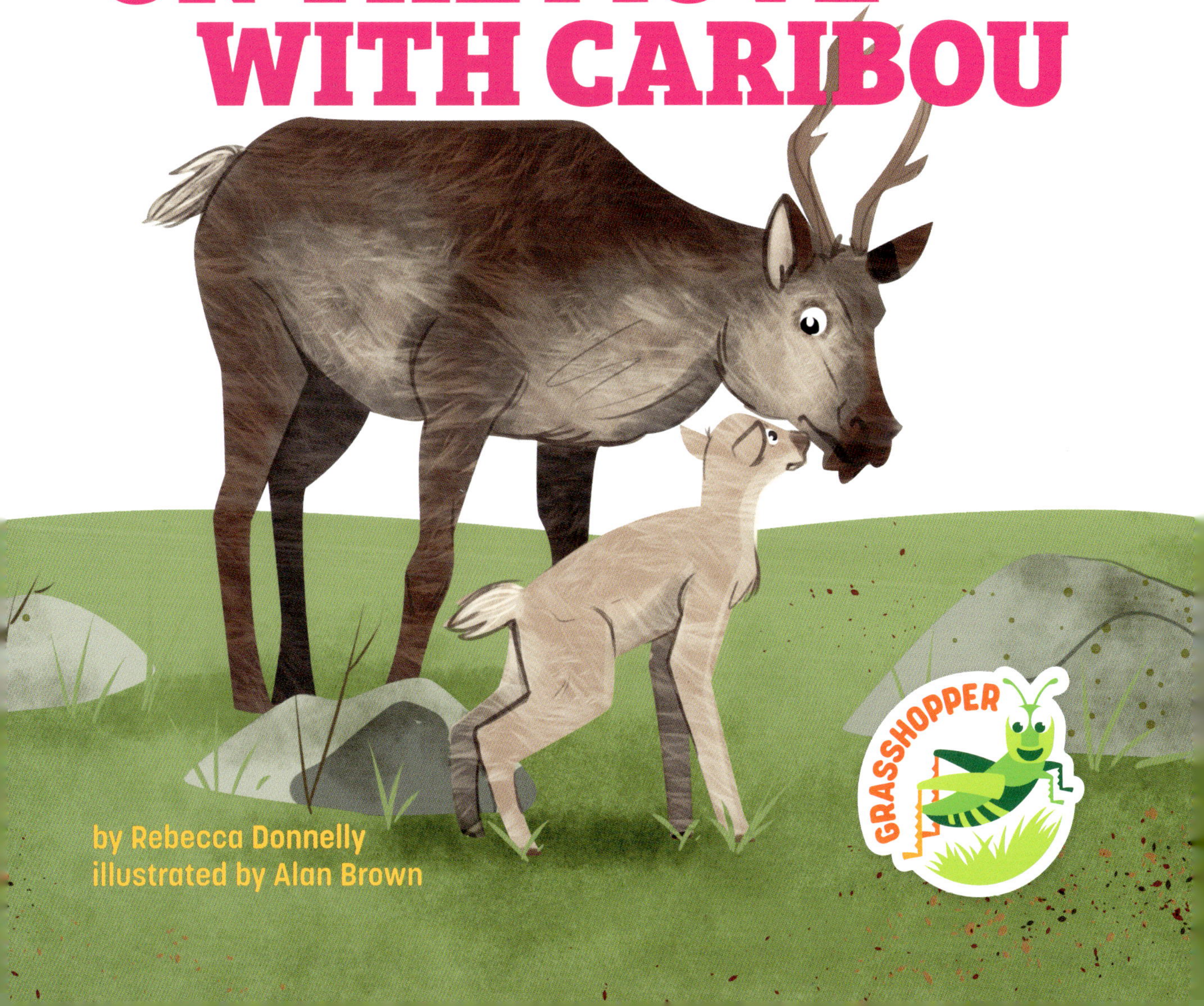

by Rebecca Donnelly
illustrated by Alan Brown

GRASSHOPPER

Tools for Parents & Teachers

Grasshopper Books enhance imagination and introduce the earliest readers to fiction with fun storylines and illustrations. The easy-to-read text supports early reading experiences with repetitive sentence patterns and sight words.

Before Reading

- Discuss the cover illustration. What do readers see?
- Look at the glossary together. Discuss the words.

Read the Book

- Read the book to the child, or have him or her read independently.
- "Walk" through the book and look at the illustrations. Who is the main character? What is happening in the story?

After Reading

- Prompt the child to think more. Ask: Carly has a thick coat and wide hooves. How do these help her migrate and live in Alaska?

Grasshopper Books are published by Jump!
5357 Penn Avenue South
Minneapolis, MN 55419
www.jumplibrary.com

Library of Congress Cataloging-in-Publication Data

Names: Donnelly, Rebecca, author.
Brown, Alan, illustrator.
Title: On the move with caribou
Rebecca Donnelly; illustrated by Alan Brown.
Description: Minneapolis, MN: Jump!, Inc., [2023]
Series: Amazing migrations | Includes index.
Audience: Ages 7-10
Identifiers: LCCN 2021060825 (print)
LCCN 2021060826 (ebook)
ISBN 9781636908793 (hardcover)
ISBN 9781636908809 (paperback)
ISBN 9781636908816 (ebook)
Subjects: LCSH: Caribou–Migration–Juvenile literature.
Migratory animals–Juvenile literature.
Classification: LCC QL737.U55 D66 2023 (print)
LCC QL737.U55 (ebook)
DDC 599.65/81568–dc23/eng/20220110
LC record available at https://lccn.loc.gov/2021060825
LC ebook record available at https://lccn.loc.gov/2021060826

Editor: Eliza Leahy
Direction and Layout: Anna Peterson
Illustrator: Alan Brown

Printed in the United States of America at
Corporate Graphics in North Mankato, Minnesota.

Table of Contents

A Long Journey

I'm Carly. I'm a caribou calf. I was born here, in northern Alaska. A lot of calves are born here every spring.

I'm only a few hours old, but I can already run. I have to move fast to keep up with my mom and the rest of the herd. There are 200,000 of us!

In summer, there are a lot of tasty plants to eat. I love blueberries and grasses!

There are a lot of mosquitoes, too. We all stay together in a big group called an aggregation. This makes it harder for mosquitoes to bite us! We also look for cool places where there aren't as many bugs.

Soon it will be fall. There won't be enough for us to eat here. That means it's time to migrate. We travel south to our winter range. We walk across mountains and plains.

We come to a river.
I have to swim across.

My wide hooves help me. But the current is strong. I can't keep up with Mama! I call out to her.

Mama hears me and comes back. She blocks the current so I can swim to the other side.

Brr! It's getting cold. Snow falls.
We'll spend winter in this forest.
My thick coat keeps me warm.

My hooves help me walk on the snow. They also help me dig for food. I smell lichen!

Uh-oh, wolves! They are looking for caribou to eat. Mama and the other adults stay on the outside of the herd. The other calves and I are safe in the middle.

It's still cold and snowy, but soon it will be spring. We move north to our summer range. It's hard work breaking through the deep snow. The cows take turns leading the way. The other calves and I follow the path they make.

The cows get to the calving area first. I follow slowly with the other yearlings. The bulls come last. It has been a long 800 miles (1,287 kilometers).

Look, a newborn calf! And there's a lot of yummy food. I can't wait to eat blueberries again after a long, cold winter!

Migration Map

In winter, caribou travel south. They return north in spring. Take a look at where Carly's herd travels!

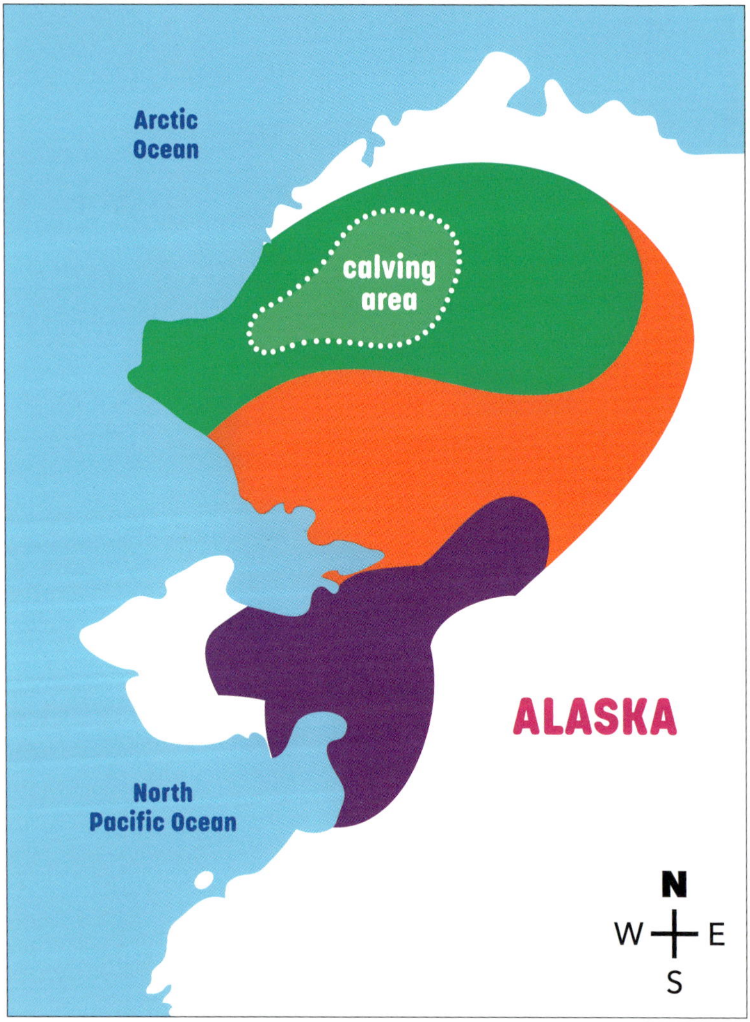

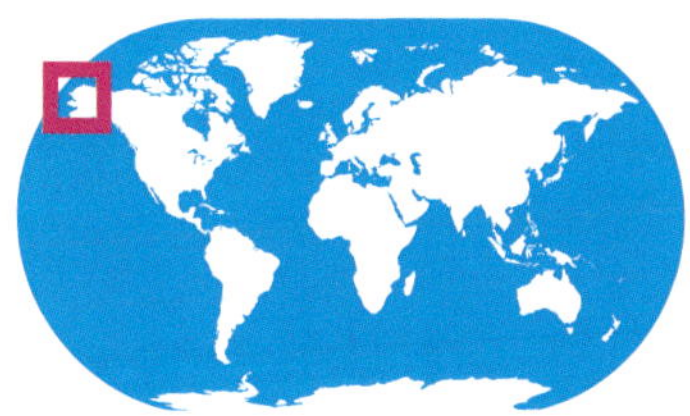

Let's Review!

Why does Carly's herd migrate to their winter range?

A. to escape wolves
B. to swim in rivers
C. to have calves
D. to find food

Glossary

aggregation: A large group of caribou that stands close together for protection.

bulls: Adult male caribou.

calf: A newborn or young caribou.

calving area: The area where female caribou give birth to their calves.

cows: Adult female caribou.

current: The movement of water in a definite direction in a river or ocean.

herd: A large group of caribou that lives and migrates together.

hooves: The hard parts of the feet of some animals such as caribou.

lichen: Flat algae and fungi that grow on rocks and trees.

migrate: To move from one area to another at certain times of the year.

range: The area in which an animal or plant lives.

yearlings: Caribou calves that are between one and two years old.

Index

To Learn More

Finding more information is as easy as 1, 2, 3.

1. Go to www.factsurfer.com
2. Enter "**onthemovewithcaribou**" into the search box.
3. Choose your book to see a list of websites.